Written by Hannah Wilson.
Illustrations by Chris Dickason.
Cover typography based on designs by Thy Bui.

First published in Great Britain in 2023 by Red Shed, part of Farshore

An imprint of HarperCollins*Publishers*
1 London Bridge Street, London SE1 9GF
www.farshore.co.uk

HarperCollins*Publishers*
Macken House, 39/40 Mayor Street Upper,
Dublin 1, D01 C9W8, Ireland

Copyright © HarperCollins*Publishers* Limited 2023

ISBN 978-0-00-861222-1

Printed and bound in the UK using 100% Renewable Electricity at CPI Group (UK) Ltd.

001

A CIP catalogue record for this title is available from the British Library.

MIX
Paper | Supporting
responsible forestry
FSC™ C007454

This book is produced from independently certified FSC™ paper
to ensure responsible forest management.

For more information visit: www.harpercollins.co.uk/green

AMAZING FACTS

SIR DAVID ATTENBOROUGH

RED SHED

Did you know?

David changed the way
we see animals on TV.

His favourite animal is the human being.

He once came face to face
with a troop of gorillas.

He shared an island with 120 million crabs.

David is a champion of the Earth.

Read on to discover over 100 fascinating and surprising facts about Sir David Attenborough, his childhood, his TV career and his extraordinary wildlife encounters!

Sir David Attenborough was born in London, UK, on 8th May 1926.

The much-loved naturalist (someone who studies living things) is known all over the world for making awe-inspiring wildlife documentaries.

David has been on TV for a record-breaking 70 years.

No one has been a TV naturalist – or presenter – for so long! Since he first presented *Animal Disguises*, a children's TV programme, in 1953, the hard-working naturalist has made more than 800 TV programmes.

David is a knight ... twice over!

He was given a knighthood by Queen Elizabeth II at Buckingham Palace in 1985, proudly watched by his wife, Jane, and daughter, Susan. Arise, Sir David!

In 2022, aged 96, David was given a second knighthood for his services to broadcasting and conservation.

David's favourite animal is the human being!

He is particularly fond of 'absolutely fascinating' nine-month-old babies!

But his favourite non-human animal is a monkey!

David says they're fun and funny! What's your favourite animal?

**If David could be any animal
in the world, he'd be a sloth!**

**There's only one animal
David doesn't like . . .**

David is not a fan of rats. A rat ran up his leg
once when he was sitting on a toilet in India. Eek!

As a boy, David loved to hunt for fossils.

He would cycle around the countryside near his home in Leicestershire, looking for bird nests, dragonflies and snakes. He'd wrap any fossils he found in newspaper and take them home in his bike bag.

David once sold newts for three pence each.

When David was about 11 years old, he caught newts in a nearby pond and sold them to the zoology department at University College Leicester. They gave him three pence for every newt – which was worth about £15 back then! A newt looks like a small lizard, but it's actually an amphibian – it can live on both land and in water.

Beavers and a grey owl once inspired David.

Strange but true! Grey Owl was the nickname of an environmentalist called Archibald Belaney. Ten-year-old David listened wide-eyed when he gave a lecture in 1936 about saving the beaver and its home in the Canadian wilderness.

David once made buttons in a factory.

David was 13 when World War II broke out in 1939. Many women and young people worked in factories during that time. Later, the nature-lover would describe making plastic buttons as the worst job he had ever had!

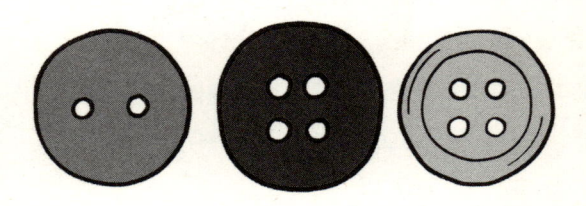

During the war, David's family looked after two young Jewish refugees.

Sisters Irene and Helga Bejach had fled Berlin, Germany, arriving in the UK before the war broke out. They lived with the Attenborough family for seven years and were eventually adopted by David's parents, Frederick and Mary.

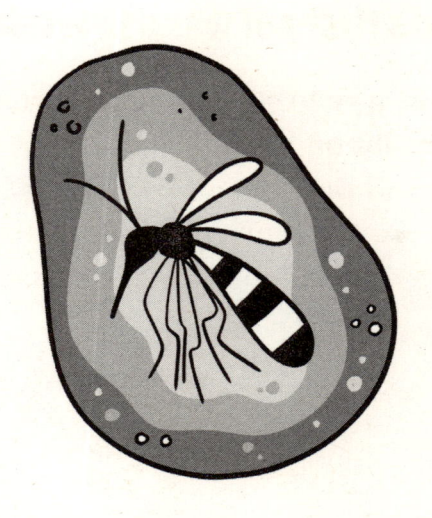

David made a TV documentary about a piece of amber he had kept for more than 60 years.

The golden lump of fossilized tree resin (sticky stuff that's found inside trees) was a gift from another Jewish refugee, 12-year-old Marianne, who came to live with the Attenboroughs in 1938. The amber helped inspire David's interest in the natural world.

David's first pet was a fire salamander.

He was given the amphibian by his father as a present on his eighth birthday. He fed it slugs and worms, and kept it in a large tank. It often escaped!

David gave his own son, Richard, a fire salamander on *his* eighth birthday. Salamanders can live for up to 50 years in captivity.

David studied rocks and animals at university.

Along with his brothers, Richard and John, David went to Wyggeston Grammar School for Boys in Leicester. Later, David studied studied geology and zoology as part of his Natural Sciences degree at the University of Cambridge.

David didn't even own a television when he started working in TV!

David started working at the BBC (British Broadcasting Corporation) as a trainee in 1952. Until then, he had only watched one TV programme in his whole life – and the only people he knew who had a TV were the parents of his wife, Jane.

David learned how to operate a TV camera.

As a BBC trainee, David was taught a range of skills. At that time, TV cameras were large metal boxes mounted on bicycle wheels. Today, his film crew use the latest technology: remote cameras and drones (small flying devices).

David was turned down for the first BBC job he applied for!

When David applied to be a BBC radio producer, he received a rejection letter in the post. Better luck next time, David!

David helped make a TV show about a prehistoric fish!

In 1952, a live coelacanth (a prehistoric fish previously thought to be extinct) was discovered in the Indian Ocean. David found a fossilized coelacanth and some sharks that had been pickled (preserved in chemicals) for the presenter to talk about on the show.

David helped make a programme about knitting.

It's true! After spending time as a trainee, David was given a job in the BBC's Talks Department. As an assistant producer, he helped make programmes on topics as varied as knitting, ballet, gardening, politics, archaeology, and more!

David changed the way we see animals on TV.

In the 1950s and 60s, it was mostly zoo animals that appeared on TV. The creatures were removed from their cages at night, then taken to a brightly lit studio. David wanted to make a TV series where cameras travelled to animals' natural habitats instead.

David's first TV show was called *Zoo Quest*.

When Jack Lester, a reptile keeper at London Zoo, invited David to Sierra Leone, in Africa, to find snakes and other creatures, David jumped at the chance. Together they came up with the idea for a new show, *Zoo Quest*, recording the expedition on film.

Today, zoos understand the importance of not removing animals from their natural habitats.

David became a TV presenter by accident.

When they returned from Africa, Jack became ill. David had to present the studio sections of *Zoo Quest*. It was 1954 and a TV star was born!

Every episode of the first *Zoo Quest* series featured the hunt for a crow!

David and Jack were looking for a type of crow called *Picathartes*, or bald crow, which was rare and had never been filmed before. Helped by villagers in Sierra Leone, they finally found the elusive white-necked birds.

David met a chimp called Jane.

On their expedition to Sierra Leone, David and Jack met a host of creatures, including Jane, a young chimp, a mongoose, a Gaboon viper, bush rats, an antelope, owls, sun birds and a ground squirrel.

David fed the squirrel palm nuts and placed a little bottle of hot water nearby to keep it warm at night.

Today, naturalists know that it's best to just watch wild animals, rather than touch and play with them.

David patted a toothy capybara.

Filming for *Zoo Quest* in Guyana, South America, David was thrilled to meet a special village pet. Capybaras are the world's largest rodent. Rodents' teeth never stop growing – and they have to gnaw continually to shorten them!

David once ate a hairy moth caterpillar.

In New Guinea, David munched on this local delicacy. He burnt off its hairs first by roasting the bug on a fire. Er, yum?

David tried to catch a giant anteater.

When the large animal turned around and showed David its powerful claws, used for ripping apart termite mounds, David wisely gave up the chase!

David travelled to Indonesia to look for dragons.

Not the mythical beast, though! In 1954, David went on an expedition to look for real-life giant lizards: Komodo dragons. These fearsome reptiles are 3m long and kill their prey with a poisonous bite. Yikes!

Zoo Quest didn't get a permit to take a dragon back to the UK. The lucky lizard could stay on Komodo Island, its home. Nowadays, naturalists avoid taking creatures out of the natural habitats where they belong.

David got caught in a whirlpool!

On the expedition to Komodo Island, David's sailing boat was swept onto a coral reef and into a series of whirlpools! David used bamboo poles to help push the boat to safety. The whole voyage was difficult – the captain didn't know where the island was, and there was no equipment to catch fish for food!

David once wrestled a crocodile.

When David spotted the gharial crocodile
in a river in Borneo, he took off his shirt and,
using it as a net, dived towards the scaly beast.
Super scary! Erm, not really – it was only a baby,
about 50cm long!

Today gharials – also known as fish-eating
crocodiles – are critically endangered
because of hunting and damage to
their environment caused by humans.

David saved some rare lemurs.

He dismantled a hunter's trap to prevent the rare brown Madagascan lemurs, nestled in nearby trees, from becoming ensnared. Lifesaver!

David met some
record-breaking tenrecs.

The naturalist brought a few of these small hedgehog-like creatures back from Madagascar. The tenrec holds the official record for the most wild mammal babies born in one go: 31. Imagine having 30 brothers and sisters!

David completed an eggs-tremely difficult jigsaw puzzle!

About 1,000 years ago, *Aepyornis*, a 3m-tall flightless 'elephant bird' roamed Madagascar, Africa. When David visited the island in 1960 for another *Zoo Quest* episode, he taped together fragments of an ancient *Aepyornis* eggshell. The egg was huge – about 30cm long, roughly the volume of 160 chicken eggs!

David loved his knee-high socks!

The young naturalist always looked tip-top even in the wilderness. He wore a khaki-coloured shirt tucked into his shorts, smart shoes with socks pulled up to the knees, and hair neatly combed with a side parting.

In later years, David travelled with eight identical blue shirts.

He also packed four pairs of khaki trousers. Why? So he could always look the same in every scene, no matter where he was and when it was filmed!

A gibbon, a cockatoo, parrots and a lungfish have all lived with David.

When London Zoo couldn't house all the animals David collected, he often looked after them in his own home!

David kept poisonous dart frogs.

It's true! Some indigenous people from the rainforests of South America rub dart tips over the skin of these frogs. After soaking up the powerful toxins, the darts are used for hunting, blown through tubes towards animal prey.

A woolly monkey once lived in David's house.

William was a jealous little monkey. When David's young daughter, Susan, sat on his lap, William would try to squeeze in between them!

David's curtains smelt of bushbaby wee!

David looked after several bushbabies in his house. To make themselves feel at home, they liked to wee on their hands and wipe it all over the curtains and furniture. That must have smelt wee-ly bad!

David saved an orphaned baby bear.

In 1956, while filming *Zoo Quest*, David met a week-old Malaysian sun bear cub who had lost his mother. David and his cameraman, Charles, looked after the hungry little bear, feeding him milk from a bottle. They named him Benjamin.

When he flew home, David took Benjamin on the plane with him. Back in the UK, Benjamin stayed with Charles in his flat. He ripped all the carpets and scratched all the furniture! Oops!

Nowadays, naturalists try to take care of vulnerable animals in their own habitats.

David's biggest battle is against climate change.

Working with top scientists, David has made many nature programmes that show the devastating impacts of human-made global warming on our wild spaces. He has told viewers about problems such as deforestation and disappearing ice caps, and he works hard to find solutions, such as creating wildlife reserves.

"What happens next is up to every one of us."
– Sir David Attenborough

David is an official Champion of the Earth.

In 2022, the United Nations recognised David as a Champion of the Earth. For many years, he has fought to protect our planet and its inhabitants.

David once talked about climate change with Greta Thunberg.

A meeting of mighty planet-savers, young and old! Put on your green superhero capes!

Blue Planet II was watched by over 14 million people in the UK.

Viewers in the UK were glued to their TVs as David presented this 2017 series about the Earth's oceans.

After the programme aired, internet searches about saving ocean creatures rocketed. People were shocked when *Blue Planet II* showed a turtle trapped in a plastic sack. Many people turned shock into action and decided to use less plastic.

David said: "Look after the natural world. It's the most precious thing we have."

A walrus mum and pup nearly made David cry.

The exhausted mum and her baby, swimming in the Arctic Ocean, couldn't find any ice to rest on.

David was upset to witness the effect of global heating, which has reduced the Arctic's sea ice dramatically.

David once rescued a pangolin from a hunter.

He paid the hunter some money for it and later set it free. All species of pangolin are critically endangered.

David's team met the last two northern white rhinos.

Mother and daughter Najin and Fatu live on the Ol Pejeta Conservancy in Kenya, East Africa. They are the last surviving members of their species, which has been wiped out by hunting and habitat loss.

"Only now do I realise just how lucky I've been - many of these wonders seem set to disappear for ever." – Sir David Attenborough

The world's population is about four times larger than it was when David was born.

There are now eight billion of us on this planet. It's no wonder David is worried that humans are taking up too much of the natural wildernesses that plants and animals need to survive.

The animal David most wishes he could save from extinction is the black lion tamarin.

These small, maned monkeys live in Brazil, and there are only about 1,600 adults left. Like many endangered animals, this tamarin is threatened by loss of habitat – its forest home is being cut down to make fields for farming.

A coral reef gave David his most amazing nature experience ever.

David will never forget the first time he went scuba-diving on the Great Barrier Reef in 1957. Surrounded by colourful fish, and creatures he didn't even know existed, he called it "the most beautiful sight in the whole of the natural world".

David returned to the Great Barrier Reef 60 years later and found that it had been bleached white by warmer seas. The world's reefs are in huge danger from climate change, pollution and over-fishing.

David lay next to the largest turtle in the world.

It's turtle-ly true! One night, David lay on a beach on a Caribbean island and watched quietly as a leatherback turtle prepared to lay her eggs in the sand. These giant reptiles can measure up to 2m long and weigh about half a tonne– that's as much a horse or cow!

David met Lonesome George.

Lonesome George was thought to be the last remaining giant tortoise on Pinta Island in the Galapagos Islands. David spent time with him just ten days before he died in 2012. David has campaigned tirelessly to protect vulnerable creatures from extinction.

David shared an island with 120 million crabs.

On Christmas Island, David tiptoed among a wriggling carpet of female red crabs. They were marching towards the sea, each one carrying 100,000 eggs to drop into the Indian ocean. Egg-ceptional!

David sniffed the largest flower in the world.

In the rainforest of Sumatra, Indonesia, David came across a 2.75m-tall Titan arum, the world's largest flower (although some say it is several smaller flowers joined together). Its fishy smell was so bad it made David cough. Luckily it only flowers every 1,000 days and the flower lasts for just three days!

David met a manatee with bad breath.

The plant-eating manatee swam up to David while he was snorkelling in a warm Florida river and gave a very stinky snort. Hold your nose, David!

A teddy-bear cactus once spiked David through two gloves.

Never cuddle a teddy-bear cholla cactus! Its densely packed, glass-like spines pricked David even though he was wearing two gloves on his hand. Ouch!

David dangled on a rope in a cloud of bats.

Who was that tiny figure dangling on a rope, high above the cave floor, surrounded by 200,000 free-tailed bats, heading out to feed? It was, of course, our brave naturalist, then 88 years old!

David was flabbergasted by a bird that buzzed like a chainsaw!

An amazing mimic, the lyrebird of southern Australia can copy the sounds of forest machinery, car alarms, clicking cameras and 20 different species of bird!

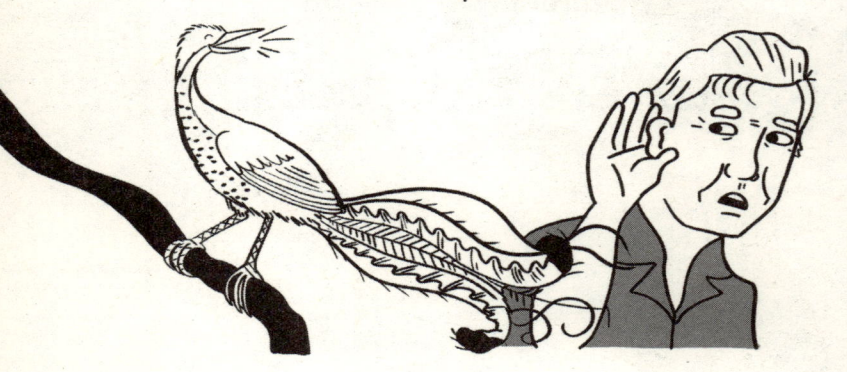

Two rocks helped David chat to a woodpecker.

In the forests of southern Argentina, David tapped two rocks on a tree to chat with a nearby red-headed woodpecker. The bird used its beak to tap back, thinking David was a rival male!

David loves birds of paradise.

David was one of the first documentary makers to film these beautiful birds. Ever since, he has been fascinated by their colourful, shimmering feathers, and the way the males dance to impress the females. It's one of the greatest nature shows on Earth!

The world's smallest reptile sat on David's finger.

The teeny-weeny dwarf chameleon, from Madagascar, was the size of his fingernail!

David found a cunning way to catch flies!

He once walked around a garden with a chameleon on his arm. When he pointed the lizard at a fly, the reptile shot out its tongue to catch it.

David and his team were the first to film a wild rattlesnake catching its prey.

The team used tracking equipment to find the snake, then set up movement-detecting cameras. Later, David was fascinated to watch the hungry rattlesnake strike and kill a mouse with one powerful bite. It was nature film hissss-tory!

David once said "boo" to a sloth!

He climbed a ladder to come face to face
with the slow-moving, tree-dwelling mammal.
Sloths have very limited eyesight and hearing,
so when David said "Boo!", the creature
barely noticed.

Once a week, a sloth slowly lowers itself to the
forest floor to have a poo. Nobody knows why it
leaves the safety of the trees just for this!

David is a master of monkey medicine.

In Costa Rica, he placed two different types of leaves on the forest floor. The nearby capuchin monkeys knew which ones to take: they chose the medicinal Piper leaves, which they rubbed all over each other to repel insects and heal infections.

But he's also a monkey mischief-maker!

David once pulled a model of a leopard
through a west African rainforest! He wasn't
terrifying the local monkeys just for fun –
he wanted to show that the monkeys make
a different alarm call for different predators.
Sound the leopard alarm!

David once sat in a deep dark cave and waited for . . . elephants.

While in Kenya, David watched elephants coming to the cave at night in search of salt, which they need to keep their bodies healthy. They scratched the salt from the cave walls with their tusks, sucked it up with their trunks and blew it into their mouths!

David knows animals feel differently from humans.

When David saw elephants touching the bones of a dead relative with their trunks, he was careful not to assume they were sad in the same way that humans would be.

David often points out that animal emotions and behaviours are completely different from those of humans – even if it's tempting to make comparisons.

David filmed rare elephant twins.

David and his team watched in surprise as mother Angelica gave birth to not one but two calves in the Amboseli National Park in Kenya. The birth of twins is very rare. The rest of the herd helped Angelica to look after babies Atlas and Alana.

David came face to face with a troop of gorillas.

One of David's most famous TV moments was filmed in the mountains of Rwanda in 1978. He spent hours with a troop of gorillas and was amazed by how gentle and human-like the powerful apes were.

A baby gorilla tried to pull his shoes off!

The young gorilla was called Poppy. David got the giggles and couldn't concentrate on what he was supposed to be saying!

One gorilla put her huge hand on David's head.

She was a gentle giant and David was totally unharmed. He later said that her hand was "as large as a boxing glove". David spent hours patiently sitting with the gorilla because he realised she could become upset if he walked away.

During the encounter, David said: "There's more meaning and mutual understanding in exchanging a glance with a gorilla than any other animal I know."

David was a brilliant belcher!

Yes, really! It's important not to surprise a gorilla, so David let out very small belches to let the troop know that he was approaching.

A grumpy grouse once knocked David over!

The black, chicken-sized bird was not happy when David stepped into its territory in the Scottish Highlands. It puffed up its feathers and charged, knocking him to the ground!

A pink iguana once attacked David's filming equipment.

The male iguana lashed out at an expensive mirror, part of the camera. Perhaps it thought the creature reflected in the glass was a rival male!

An elephant seal made David jump.

While filming in Antarctica, David had to leap out of the way as a grumpy bull elephant seal, about three tonnes in weight and 5m long, came lumbering towards him!

A rhino once rammed his jeep.

It charged out of the east African bushland and, with a mighty *boom*, hit the back of David's jeep. Then the rhino lifted up the back of the vehicle with its horns and shook it about. Luckily, David was unharmed – unlike the jeep!

David has travelled further than almost anyone on the planet . . .

For just one of his documentaries, *The Life of Birds*, broadcast in 1998, he travelled 412,000km. That's the same as travelling around the world ten times.

But David doesn't own a car.

The naturalist hasn't even got a driving licence!

David flew over the Alps in a hot-air balloon.

A comfortable flight over Europe's tallest peaks? Not really! When David is filming, it's important that no one else can be seen on camera. While David was being filmed from a helicopter hovering nearby, the rest of the team stayed hidden, crouching next to David's legs at the bottom of the basket. What a squash!

David once munched chocolates in a submarine.

In 2015, David descended 300m in the Triton submersible to see the deep-sea marine life of Australia's Great Barrier Reef. It was a record-breaking mission – no vessel had dived that deep before. David said it was like "being in a cinema" – and he even took chocolate to eat!

David floated about inside the 'vomit comet'.

That's the nickname for a plane that flies steeply up, then steeply down again. At the peak of the climb, the passengers experience weightlessness – just like astronauts in a space station. The lack of gravity can make people vomit. Thankfully, David kept his breakfast down!

David is a polar explorer.

He reached the North Pole in April 2010, coping with temperatures as low as −50°C. Only a few weeks earlier, he'd been at the South Pole. Brr!

David was boiling hot in Iceland.

That's because he was standing next to an erupting volcano. Mind the lava, David!

David once tried to solve the mystery of the Loch Ness Monster.

Really? Yes! For his 1975 show *Fabulous Animals*, David wondered if a 1933 sighting of a giant monster at the famous Scottish lake was in fact a giant eel crossing the road! That sounds eel-ly unlikely . . .

He also thinks the Yeti might be real!

The legendary Yeti, or 'Abominable Snowman', is a large, ape-like creature that is said to live in the mountains of the Himalayas. Mysterious footprints have been found thousands of metres up the snowy slopes – and David wondered if the legend might be true!

David is a dino detective.

In Argentina, David joined scientists investigating giant dinosaur bones, more than 100 million years old. The bones belonged to the largest dinosaur that ever lived, a mighty titanosaur. It was long as three double-decker buses and as tall as a five-storey building!

If David could bring any extinct creature back to life, he'd choose a pterosaur.

Yikes! In fact, he'd choose a *Quetzalcoatlus*, the largest pterosaur of all time. This prehistoric flying reptile had a wingspan of more than 11m, the size of a small plane! Even bigger yikes!

David's big brother was a dino movie star!

Richard Attenborough (1923–2014) starred in the 1993 blockbuster movie *Jurassic Park*! Richard was a famous actor and filmmaker. He was also in the 1967 film *Doctor Dolittle*, hanging out with animals – just like his little brother!

Attenborosaurus was a prehistoric marine reptile.

Named after David, the long-necked, flippered beast swam in our seas about 190 million years ago. This is one Jurassic creature that didn't make it into the movie!

The earliest-known predator is also named after David.

Auroralumina attenboroughii was not a fearsome dinosaur, an ancient shark or a ferocious cave bear. The 560-million-year-old predator was more like, erm, a jellyfish!

David has given his name to more than 50 plants and creatures.

These include lizards, wasps, goblin spiders, songbirds, ghost shrimps, flatworms, weevils, frogs, beetles and bats. He has even given his name to *Nepenthes attenboroughii*, a carnivorous plant! You wouldn't want that one in your bathroom!

David was friends with Queen Elizabeth II.

David and the late Queen Elizabeth were both born in 1926, within a couple of weeks of each other, and they spent time together on several occasions over the years.

David first met King Charles in 1958.

The future king and his younger sister, Anne, visited the BBC studios in 1958. David introduced them to his cockatoo, 'Cocky'!

David's face was projected onto Buckingham Palace!

It's true! The naturalist was giving a speech outside the palace as part of the Jubilee celebrations in June 2022, marking the Queen's 70 years on the throne.

There's a ship called
Sir David Attenborough.

The Antarctic research ship was named in 2016 in honour of David's 90th birthday. The ship was almost called *Boaty McBoatface* after the public voted for this funny name. *Boaty McBoatface* became the name of one of the ship's small submersibles instead!

David was king of colour TV.

In 1965, David was put in charge of BBC2.
Two years later, in 1967, under David's leadership,
BBC2 became the first UK TV channel to
broadcast in colour! Before this, all shows
appeared in black and white.

After introducing colour TV, David realised that
snooker, with its coloured balls, could now be
shown on the telly. The snooker show *Pot Black*
made the sport popular with TV viewers.

David is a record-breaking award winner.

He's the only person to have won BAFTA (British Academy of Film and Television Arts) awards for shows broadcast on black-and-white, colour, HD (high-definition) and 3D (three-dimensional) television!

No one has more honorary degrees from British universities than David.

His 32 degrees recognise his amazing contribution to the natural world, helping to explain it and to protect it. What's the best thing about honorary degrees? There's no need to study or take an exam!

Meerkats United **was once voted the best wildlife documentary of all time.**

This 1987 *Wildlife on One* episode followed a mob of meerkats in the Kalahari Desert, southern Africa, as they encountered snakes and jackals, kept watch over their desert home and wrestled with each other!

David saw a surprising sight on the slopes of Mount Kinabalu.

While walking down from Borneo's highest peak, he bumped into a lady who showed him something totally unexpected – a tattoo of Sir David Attenborough on her leg. David came face to face with his own face!

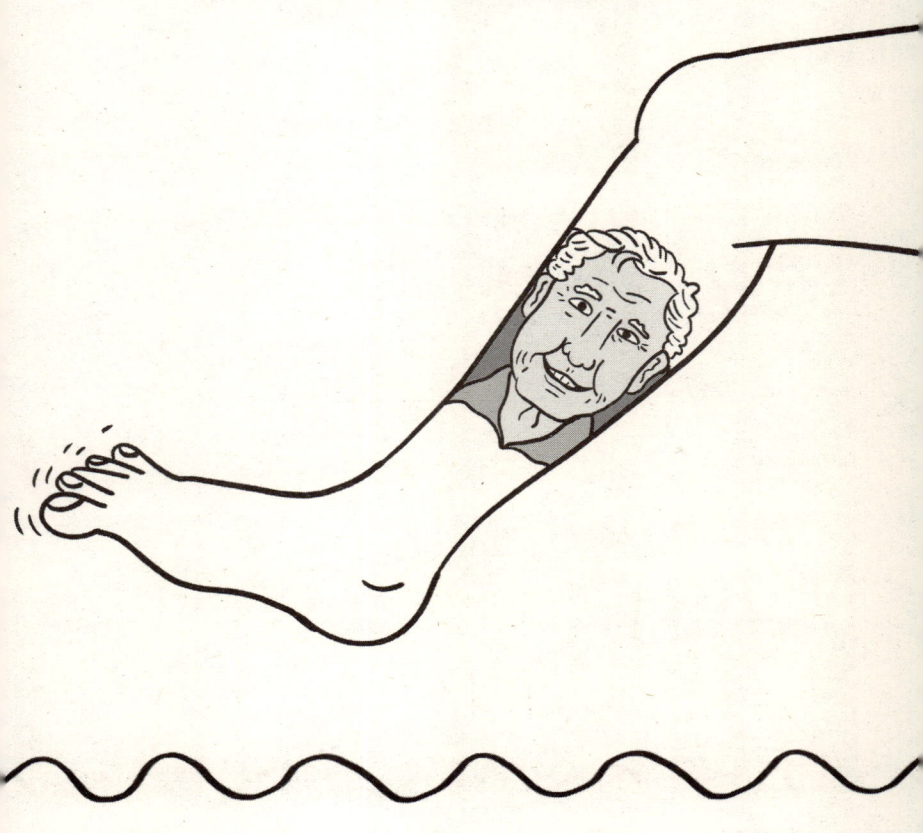

Look out for other books in the series!

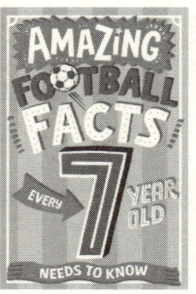